The Belle of Amherst

The Belle of Amherst

A Play based on the Life of
EMILY DICKINSON

by

William Luce

As produced on the stage by
Mike Merrick and Don Gregory

HOUGHTON MIFFLIN COMPANY
BOSTON

Library of Congress Cataloging in Publication Data

Luce, William.
    The belle of Amherst.

    1. Dickinson, Emily, 1830-1886, in fiction, drama, poetry, etc. I. Title.
PS3562.U254B4   812'.5'4   76-41226
ISBN 0-395-24980-5   ISBN 0-395-26253-4 pbk.

Printed in the United States of America
CAUTION: Professionals and amateurs are hereby warned that *The Belle of Amherst,* being fully protected under the copyright laws of the United States of America, the British Empire, including the Dominion of Canada, and all other countries of the Berne and Universal Copyright Conventions, is subject to royalty. All rights, including professional, amateur, motion picture, recitation, lecturing, public readings, radio and television broadcasting, phonograph recording rights, and rights of translation into foreign languages, are strictly reserved. All inquiries regarding this play should be addressed to the author's agent,
Dome Productions
9200 Sunset Boulevard
Los Angeles, California 90069

W 10 9 8 7 6

Acknowledgments

The author gratefully acknowledges use of the following materials:

LETTERS OF EMILY DICKINSON, by Mabel Loomis Todd, © 1931.

ANCESTORS' BROCADES, by Millicent Todd Bingham, © 1945.

EMILY DICKINSON — A REVELATION, by Millicent Todd Bingham, © 1954.

BOLTS OF MELODY: NEW POEMS OF EMILY DICKINSON, by Mabel Loomis Todd and Millicent Todd Bingham, © 1945.

EMILY DICKINSON'S HOME, by Millicent Todd Bingham, © 1955.

All the foregoing copyright by The Trustees of Amherst College. All used by permission of Harper & Row, Publishers, Inc.

Materials used by permission of the Houghton Library, Harvard University:

EMILY DICKINSON FACE TO FACE, by Martha D. Bianchi, © 1932, and LIFE AND LETTERS OF EMILY DICKINSON, by Martha D. Bianchi, © 1924, are published by Houghton Mifflin Company.

THE HIDDEN LIFE OF EMILY DICKINSON, by John Walsh, © 1971, by permission of Simon & Schuster, Inc.

THE LYMAN LETTERS, by Richard B. Sewall, © 1965, through the courtesy of the University of Massachusetts Press.

THE YEARS AND HOURS OF EMILY DICKINSON, by Jay Leyda, © 1960, by permission of the Yale University Press.

SELECTIONS FROM THE UNPUBLISHED LETTERS OF EMILY DICKINSON TO HER BROTHER'S FAMILY, by Martha Bianchi, © 1915, from *The Atlantic Monthly*.

Certain poems and letters of Emily Dickinson are used by permission of Harvard University Press and The Trustees of Amherst College. They are published by the Belknap Press of Harvard University Press in THE POEMS OF EMILY DICKINSON and THE LETTERS OF EMILY DICKINSON, each edited by Thomas H. Johnson.

Texts of certain poems of Emily Dickinson appearing in the play are taken from the COMPLETE POEMS OF EMILY DICKINSON, edited by Thomas H. Johnson, © 1929 by Martha Dickinson Bianchi, © 1957 by Mary L. Hampson, by permission of Little, Brown & Company.

The author gratefully acknowledges the inspiration gained from THE LIFE OF EMILY DICKINSON, by Richard B. Sewall, published by Farrar, Straus and Giroux, 1974, New York.

Mike Merrick and Don Gregory
present

Julie Harris
in
The Belle of Amherst

A Play Based on the Life of
Emily Dickinson

by

William Luce
Compiled by Timothy Helgeson

Scenery & lighting by

Costume design by

H.R. POINDEXTER

THEONI V. ALDREDGE

Hair design by RAY IAGNOCCO

Directed by
CHARLES NELSON REILLY

A Dome/Creative Image Production

The first performance was at the Moore Egyptian Theatre in Seattle, Washington, on February 25, 1976. The play opened on Broadway on April 28, 1976, at the Longacre Theatre, after playing Seattle, Denver, Chicago, and Boston.

To Julie Harris
and Charles Nelson Reilly,
who first envisioned this work,
with love and gratitude

Me — come! My dazzled face
In such a shining place!
Me — hear! My foreign Ear
The sounds of Welcome — there!

The Saints forget
Our bashful feet —

My Holiday, shall be
That They — remember me —
My Paradise — the fame
That They — pronounce my name —

Emily Dickinson

Preface

I first became acquainted with Emily Dickinson's poetry when I was a boy in sophomore English. Years later, a friend gave me a gift of Emily's collected letters. When I read those letters, I saw more clearly into the heart of the shy woman whose poems I had loved and admired for so long. I came to know her way of balancing richness and spareness, ecstasy and despair. There is a mystical energy, an inner tone in her writings. Emily's poems and letters radiate an invisible light. It is much like looking obliquely at a star in order to see it.

When I undertook the writing of *The Belle of Amherst*, it was my hope to depict the humanity and reasonableness of Emily Dickinson's life. I say reasonableness, because I believe that she consciously elected to be what she was — a voluntary exile from village provincialism, an original New England romantic, concisely witty, heterodox in faith, alone but not lonely, "with Will to choose, or to reject."

"And I choose," she said.

In recent years, Emily's choice has been the subject of psychoanalytic studies, some of which have portrayed her as a social isolate possessed of disordered impulses and mentally alienated from reality. The strange faces of genius are enigmatic to the structured mind, probing for final answers. Causation seems as elusive as "melody or witchcraft." Emily wrote,

> Much Madness is divinest Sense —
> To a discerning Eye —

The essential Emily of my play is secretly saying to the audience, " 'Pardon my sanity.' Pardon my jubilation in Nature, my terror of midnight, my childlike wonder at love, my white renunciation. Nothing more do I ask than to share with you the ecstasy and sacrament of my life." In my play, Emily's life is presented as a deliberate covenant with Nature and Art, a premeditated channeling of creative desire. With the same mind by which she exquisitely fashioned poems of chaste brevity, Emily superbly set the timepiece of her life. She even knew when her Coachman Death would come, and sent to her cousins a last message just before she died: "Little Cousins, — Called back. Emily."

I consider the one-person play to be uniquely suited to the telling of Emily's story. She was seclusive, an individualist of the highest order. To interpolate other actors and actresses seemed unnecessary to me. I decided that Emily alone should tell her story, sharing with the audience the inner drama of a poet's consciousness in an intimate, one-to-one relationship.

I am often asked to explain the process by which I wrote *The Belle of Amherst.* It was a creative effort founded on intensive methodical research. For two years I read and reread the several biographical studies of Emily, the three-volume collection of her letters, and the three-volume variorum edition of her poems. During this study, I took extensive notes; culled dramatically workable anecdotes, poems, and excerpts from Emily's letters; catalogued them under subject headings; rearranged them in a chronological pattern; and interwove them in a conversational style, blending in my own words as seamlessly as possible, and with the cadence and color of Emily's words. Gradually, Emily's story emerged, as if she were telling it herself.

My colleagues — "The Emily Committee" we called ourselves — also pored over the Dickinson material; and their contribution to the play was wonderfully inspiring and significant. Julie Harris, Charles Nelson Reilly, and Timothy Helgeson are all Dickinson students. Particularly, Julie's familiarity with Emily resulted from years of dedicated research into her life and works; she also recorded two albums of the letters and poems for Caedmon Records. We all seemed joined together in love in this enterprise of simple beauty. We felt it for Emily, for each other, and for the play. And we feel it for the audiences who have taken our "Belle" to their hearts.

The Belle of Amherst is a love affair with language, a celebration of all that is beautiful and poignant in life. As it turns out, shy Miss Emily was writing for theater as surely as she breathed. In her every evocative phrase there is theatrical texture. On stage, the strange ways of Emily Dickinson become dramatic qualities in an arena large enough to give them the look of "divinest Sense." Thus, the theater seems a thoroughly appropriate setting for Emily's life and art, enabling actress and audience to "climb the Bars of Ecstasy" together.

William Luce

Rancho Palos Verdes, California
May 1976

The Belle of Amherst

Synopsis of Play

The entire action of the play takes place in the Dickinson household in Amherst, Massachusetts, 1845–1886.

"Characters" in the play are Emily Elizabeth Dickinson, Maggie Maher, Austin Dickinson, James Francis Billings, Abby Wood, Jennie Hitchcock, Tutor Crowell, Edward Dickinson, Mary Lyon, Lavinia Dickinson, Buffy, Susan Gilbert Dickinson, Thomas Wentworth Higginson, Charles Wadsworth, Emily Norcross Dickinson.

Act One

The curtain is always up.

The stage suggests two rooms. The backdrop depicts the silhouettes of seven trees against the sky.

Stage right is EMILY DICKINSON'S *bedroom. It contains a narrow iron bed with railings at the head and foot. At the end of the bed is a trunk. By a window seat a doll sits on the floor. Downstage are a small square table and chair at which* EMILY *does her writing. A kerosene lamp is on the table. On the floor beside the table is a carved box or chest containing* EMILY'S *finished poems.*

Stage left is the Dickinson parlor. It has a square piano of the 1850 period, settee, chair, books, table, pictures, low chest, tea cart, and hall tree.

EMILY DICKINSON *is a delicate, sensitive, and quaint woman, but with an inner strength. Her manner ranges from the childlike and whimsical to the deeply poignant.*

EMILY *enters from stage left. It is 1883. She is fifty-three years old, which in her case is not too relevant, since she appears younger than she is. Her hair is auburn, parted in the center, and pulled back. She is dressed in a simple full-length white dress with an apron over it.*

EMILY

(She enters, carrying the teapot. She calls back over her shoulder)

Yes, Vinnie, I have the tea, dear!

(She places the tea on the tea cart, then looks up wide-eyed at the AUDIENCE. *Slowly she picks up a plate with slices of dark cake on it, walks shyly downstage, and extends it to the* AUDIENCE*)*

This is my introduction. Black cake. My own special recipe.

Forgive me if I'm frightened. I never see strangers and hardly know what I say. My sister, Lavinia — she's younger than I — she says I tend to wander back and forth in time. So you must bear with me. I was born December tenth, eighteen thirty, which makes me — *fifty-three?*

Welcome to Amherst. My name is Emily Elizabeth Dickinson. Elizabeth is for my Aunt Elisabeth Currier. She's Father's sister. Oh, how the trees stand up straight when they hear Aunt Libbie's little boots come thumping into Amherst! She's the only male relative on the female side.

Dear Aunt Libbie.

But I don't use my middle name anymore — since I became a *poet.*

Professor Higginson, the literary critic, doesn't think my poems are — no matter. I've had seven poems published

— anonymously, to be sure. So you see why I prefer to introduce myself to you as a poet.

Here in Amherst, I'm known as Squire Edward Dickinson's half-cracked daughter. Well, I am! The neighbors can't figure me out. I don't cross my father's ground to any house or town. I haven't left the house for years.

> The Soul selects her own Society —
> Then — shuts the Door.

(EMILY turns to the window, still holding the cake)

Why should I socialize with village gossips? There goes one of them now — Henrietta Sweetser — everyone knows Henny. She'd even intimidate the anti-Christ. Look at her! She's strolling by the house, trying to catch a glimpse of me. Would *you* like that?

So I give them something to talk about. I dress in white all year round, even in winter. "Bridal white," Henny calls it.

(She mimics back-fence gossips)

"Dear, dear! Dresses in bridal white, she does, every day of the blessed year. Year in, year out. Disappointed in love as a girl, so I hear. Poor creature. All so very sad. And her sister, Lavinia, a spinster too. Didn't you know? Oh, yes. Stayed unmarried just to be at home and take care of Miss Emily. Two old maids in that big house. What a lonely life, to shut yourself away from good people like us."

Indeed!

You should see them come to the door, bearing gifts, craning their necks, trying to see over Vinnie's shoulder. But I'm too fast for them. I've already run upstairs two steps at a time. And I hide there until they leave. You can imagine what they make of that!

One old lady came to the door the other day to get a peek inside. I surprised her by answering the door myself. She stammered something about looking for a house to buy.

(Mischievously)

To spare the expense of moving, I directed her to the cemetery.

(EMILY suddenly realizes that she is still holding the cake)

Oh! The cake!

I do all the baking here at Homestead. I even banged the spice for this cake. My father always raved about my baking. He would eat no cake or bread but mine.

(She samples a piece of cake)

Mm. Lovely.

No, no — it's easy to make. The recipe? Of course. It's really very simple. Now, I'll go slowly.

(She places the cake on the tea cart)

BLACK CAKE: two pounds of flour, two pounds of sugar,

two pounds of butter, nineteen eggs, five pounds of raisins, one and a half pounds of currants, one and a half pounds of citron, one half pint of brandy — I never use Father's best — one half pint of molasses, two nutmegs, five teaspoons of cloves, mace, and cinnamon, and — oh, yes, two teaspoons of soda, and one and a half teaspoons of salt.

(EMILY *has removed her apron*)

Just beat the butter and sugar together, add the nineteen eggs, one at a time — now this is very important — *without beating*. Then, beat the mixture again, adding the brandy alternately with the flour, soda, spices, and salt that you've sifted together. Then the molasses. Now, take your five pounds of raisins, and three pounds of currants and citron, and gently sprinkle in all eight pounds — slowly now — as you stir. Bake it for three hours if you use cake pans. If you use a milk pan, as I do, you'd better leave it in the oven six or seven hours.

Everybody *loves* it. I hope you will too. Thank you.

(*She hangs her apron on the back of the chair. Then she sits down and pours tea*)

Sometimes I bake one for a neighbor and I enclose a short note that is usually so obscure . . .

(*Gleefully*)

. . . no one can understand it! I hear my little notes are becoming collectors' items in the village. People compare them to see who has the strangest one.

Excuse me . . .

(She writes a note)

"We must be careful what we say. No bird resumes its egg."

That'll keep them guessing! Oh, that reminds me — I must send a note to Mrs. Hills. She's just been admitted to the Maplewood Infirmary . . .

(EMILY reads aloud as she writes)

> Surgeons must be very careful
> When they take the knife!
> Underneath their fine incisions
> Stirs the Culprit — *Life!*

That'll cheer her up.

I'm told one woman in Amherst is imitating me now. Probably Clarissa Cartwright. Just what Amherst needs — another eccentric.

Oh, I do have fun with them! My menagerie.

I guess people in small towns must have their local characters. And for Amherst, that's what I am. But do you know something?

(Confidentially)

I enjoy the game. I've never said this to anyone before,

but I'll tell *you*. I do it on purpose. The white dress, the seclusion. It's all — deliberate.

(She moves downstage and sits on the low chest)

But my brother, Austin — he knows. He says, "Emily! Stop your posing!"

Austin knows me through and through, as no one else does. Father and Mother never understood me. And Vinnie — Vinnie doesn't know me either. Austin and I are unlike most everyone, and are therefore more dependent on each other for delight. But — I do think — sometimes — the stories about me distress him.

In a way, the stories are true. Oh, I believe in truth. But I think it can be *slanted* just a little. Do you know what I'm saying?

> Tell all the Truth but tell it slant —
> Success in Circuit lies
> Too bright for our infirm Delight
> The Truth's superb surprise
>
> As Lightning to the Children eased
> With explanation kind
> The Truth must dazzle gradually
> Or every man be blind —

(EMILY moves to the parlor chair)

Words are my life. I look at words as if they were entities, sacred beings. There are words to which I lift my hat when I see them sitting on a page. Sometimes I write one . . .

(EMILY writes "circumference" on a paper and holds it up to be seen)

"Circumference" . . .

. . . and I look at its outlines until it starts to glow brighter than any sapphire. I hesitate which word to take when I write a poem. A poet can choose but a few words, and they have to be the chiefest words, the best words.

> A word is dead
> When it is said,
> Some say.
> I say it just
> Begins to live
> That day.

If I read Keats, Shelley, Shakespeare, Mrs. Browning, Emily Brontë — oh, what an afternoon for heaven, when Brontë entered there! — and they make my whole body so cold, no fire can ever warm me, I know that is poetry. Have you ever felt that way?

If I feel physically as if the top of my head were taken off, I know *that* is poetry. These are the only ways I know it. Is there any other way?

My friend Helen Jackson — oh, you'd love her — she's moved to Colorado — Helen is a fine scholar of words and a well-known writer. She has the facts, but not the phosphorescence.

Oh. *Phosphorescence.*

(She writes it down)

Now, there's a word to lift your hat to. Can you spell it?

To find that phosphorescence, that light within, that's the genius behind poetry.

We have an Irish girl who's been with us for a long time. I was here yesterday at tea and she asked me how to spell "genius."

(Conversing)

Why do you ask, Maggie? No, just leave the tray, dear. Oh, writing to your brother. I see. And whom are you describing?

(She gestures to herself)

Me? Oh, Maggie! Well, I guess I'd better spell it for you. G — E — N — I — U — S. Genius.

Oh, don't ask me that! I don't know what it means. No one knows that, Maggie. No one.

Thank you, dear.

(She rises and addresses the AUDIENCE)

Do you know that every one of you is, to me, a poem? You, and you — each one, a rare creation. I suppose that's why I love you and you love me, whether we realize it or not. I discovered that secret a long time ago about the souls of people.

(She comes downstage)

And I thought that *being* a poem oneself precluded the writing of poems, but I saw my mistake. The poet lights the lamp and then goes out himself. But the light goes on — and on. Essences are marked for — no, that's not the best word. *Labeled!* That's better. Essences are *labeled* for immortality.

> If I can stop one Heart from breaking
> I shall not live in vain
> If I can ease one Life the Aching
> Or cool one Pain
>
> Or help one fainting Robin
> Unto his Nest again
> I shall not live in Vain.

People find it hard to believe that I had a normal childhood. They visualize instead a miniature version of me as I am now, a pint-sized little Emily, dressed all in white, lisping riddles and aphorisms in baby talk — and of course, hiding from the family.

I guess I'm to blame for that false impression.

Actually, at fifteen, I was a very typical Amherst girl. I went to dances. I giggled my way through classes, quilting bees, and scores of parties. I was trying very hard to believe I was a ravishing beauty. I was infatuated with one dashing young man after another. Unfortunately, they didn't know it. If they did, they were smarter than I gave them credit for.

And I sent valentines.

(EMILY *sits at her desk and converses with* AUSTIN)

Austin.

Austin!

How many valentines has my handsome brother received?

Eleven?

(Annoyed)

I haven't received any! Vinnie's received some beautiful ones, but I've almost lost hope. Austin! Come in here.

(She holds up two valentines)

Which do you prefer? Do you think the heart's too big?

The cupids?

Austin. Do you think you could — tell Thomas that I'm simply pining away for a valentine? Well, surely he hasn't lost his former affection for me.

(Plaintively)

Well, why can't you?

Well, there you stand with eleven valentines, eleven! And your highly accomplished and gifted sister has been entirely overlooked!

Oh, why can't you? Please?

(She rises from the desk)

Austin, come back! What are brothers for?

(EMILY returns to her desk and proceeds to write)

"Oh, Abiah! My dearest girlfriend! Will *you* be my valentine? I would love to send you a bouquet if I had an opportunity, and you could press it and write under it, 'The Last Flowers of Summer.' Wouldn't it be poetical? And you know, that is what young ladies aim to be nowadays — poetical.

"I am growing handsome very fast, indeed.

(EMILY picks up a fan and poses with it)

"I expect I shall be the Belle of Amherst when I reach my seventeenth year. I don't doubt that I shall have perfect crowds of admirers at that age. Then, at dances, how I shall delight to make them await my bidding, and with what delight shall I witness their suspense while I make my *final decision!*"

Why, James Francis Billings! Excuse me, Mother.

(EMILY sweeps into the parlor)

What handsome whiskers! How have you been?

Isn't this a wonderful party?

Oh, thank you! It's a *Godey's Lady's Book* pattern.

I'm well, thank you!

(She sits at his invitation)

Oh, thank you!

Yes, isn't it? July is such a *glorious* month!

(She flutters her fan)

Oh, yes, delicious refreshments. Did you sample the rhubarb cupcakes? I baked them myself.

Oh. You don't like rhubarb. Well, a lot of people don't like rhubarb, I guess.

Oh my, yes! I *adore* cooking. I can't get enough of cooking. Mother says any man I marry will . . .

My sister? Oh — Lavinia is well.

Yes, I'll tell her.

(She rises and moves downstage center, as if trying to detain him)

Uh, Mr. Billings. How do you like going to school at Ipswich Seminary? Mr. Billings . . .

(To herself)

It seems Mr. Billings found the pretty girl in yellow.

(EMILY returns to the parlor and puts on her shawl)

Father's house and my garden — this is my world. And for my companions I have the hills and the sundown and my dog, Carlo, large as myself, that my father bought me. They're better than beings, because *they know*, but don't tell. And the noise in the pool at noon excels my piano.

You see, I've never had to go anywhere to find my paradise. I found it all right here — the only world I wanted — here in Amherst, Massachusetts.

Massachusetts.

Now there's a word to lift your hat to!

(She is now downstage center)

Paradise is no journey, because it's within. But for that very cause, it's the most arduous of journeys. I travel the road into my soul all the time.

> I dwell in Possibility —
> A fairer House than Prose —
> More numerous of Windows —
> Superior — for Doors —
>
> Of Chambers as the Cedars —
> Impregnable of Eye —
> And for an Everlasting Roof
> The Gables of the Sky —
>
> Of Visitors — the fairest —
> For Occupation — This —
> The spreading wide my narrow Hands
> To gather Paradise —

Nature is the highest art, don't you think? Why, just to see the summer sky is poetry.

Summer.

The orchard is full of bluejays. To see them follow the hose for a drop of water is a touching sight. They won't take it if I hand it to them. They run and shriek as if they were being assassinated. But oh, to *steal* it! That is bliss!

In June, without fail, the circus comes to town. It passed the house last night. I watched it until half-past three in the morning. Vinnie, Vinnie! Maggie! The wagons! It's here! Tell Maggie!

(EMILY runs to her bedroom and sits on the window seat)

Oh — they said, "Hoy, hoy!" to their horses. Still I feel the red in my mind, though the drums are gone.

For a while, Algiers was outside my bedroom window. Yes, *Algiers*.

I've never seen such heat. The sun beat down so today, I think everything will get ripe so it can be autumn tomorrow.

(She goes to her desk and gathers up some books)

Oh, how I loved the beginning of school each year! My girlfriends and I had such times together. Abiah Root, Sarah Tracy, Abby Wood, Emeline Kellogg, Emily Fow-

ler. There were so many Emilys at the Academy, our
teachers couldn't keep us straight.

(She balances a book on her head)

Social graces with Miss Woodbridge. "Knees straight,
girls! Shoulders back! Very good, Miss Dickinson."

(EMILY curtsies)

Thank you, Miss Woodbridge.

During my last semester, we girls formed a Shakespeare
Society. It was *my* idea.

(She walks to the parlor)

We invited the boys to join. *That* was my idea too. And
at our first meeting, we were to read *The Tempest*.

(EMILY curtsies)

Good afternoon, Tutor Crowell.

*(EMILY sits and greets her classmates. She opens her book,
pencil poised — as she slowly comprehends what the
teacher is saying)*

You want us to take all our copies and cross out the questionable passages? What do you mean *questionable*, Mr.
Crowell?

(She stands)

Decency? But what good is crossing them out going to do? I've already read them, and so has Abby. And Jennie. Haven't you, girls? Anyway, how do we dare edit Shakespeare, Mr. Crowell?

(Indignantly)

Well, I disagree! In *Hamlet* it says, "There is nothing either good or bad, but thinking makes it so."

Besides, I don't want marks in my book.

All right, all right, you boys can do as you like. But we girls don't think there's anything wicked in Shakespeare, and if there is, we don't want to know about it. *We* shall read *everything*, Mr. Crowell — naughty words and all! Come on, girls!

(EMILY opens the book and reads aloud)

"Monster, I do smell all horse-piss;
at which my nose is in great indignation."

(She kneels dramatically)

"Come to my woman's breasts,
And take my milk for gall, you murth'ring ministers."

(She now imitates HAMLET and OPHELIA)

"Lady, shall I lie in your lap?
No, my lord.
I mean my head upon your lap?
Ay, my lord.

Do you think I meant country matters?
I think nothing, my lord.
That's a fair thought to lie between maids' legs.
What is, my lord?
Nothing."

(EMILY stands on the low chest)

   "What was thy cause?
Adultery?
Thou shalt not die: die for adultery! No:
The wren goes to 't, and the small gilded fly
Does lecher in my sight.
Let copulation thrive!"

How do you like *that*, Mr. Crowell?

(EMILY is distracted by the clock)

This clock stopped this afternoon during a . . .

(The mood changes. She stops and listens)

Do you hear those bells? That's the First Congregational Church. A funeral.

(She steps down)

It must be Jennie Hitchcock's mother.

So there's one orphan more. Vinnie went to the service. Just got back. She said while the minister prayed, a hen with her chicks came up and tried to fly into the window. I suppose the dead lady used to feed them, and they wanted to bid her goodbye.

(EMILY sits and cuts fabric)

I don't know why it is, but it doesn't seem to me that I shall ever cease to live on earth. I can't imagine with the farthest stretch of my imagination my own death scene.

> This Me — that walks and works — must die,
> Some fair or stormy Day.

It's not that I'm afraid to die. Death is an old friend to me. I made his acquaintance in my childhood. So many friends died young and were carried past our house to the burial ground. Ellen Mary Kingman, the Packard girls, Abby Ann Haskell . . .

(She pauses)

. . . James Francis Billings — who didn't like rhubarb.

> There's been a Death, in the Opposite House,
> As lately as Today —
> I know it, by the numb look
> Such Houses have — alway —
>
> The Neighbors rustle in and out —
> The Doctor — drives away —
> A Window opens like a Pod —
> Abrupt — mechanically —
>
> Somebody flings a Mattress out —
> The Children hurry by —
> They wonder if it died — on that —
> I used to — when a Boy —
>
> The Minister — goes stiffly in —
> As if the House were His —

And He owned all the Mourners — now —
And little Boys, besides —

And then the Milliner — and the Man
Of the Appalling Trade —
To take the measure of the House —

There'll be that Dark Parade —

Of Tassels — and of Coaches — soon —
It's easy as a Sign —
The Intuition of the News —
In just a Country Town —

Poor Jennie.

Now, what was I telling you? Oh, yes — the clock stopped this afternoon during a thunder shower. Made it seem like Judgment Day.

I never knew how to tell time by the clock till I was fifteen. Father thought he had taught me, but I didn't understand. And I was afraid to say I didn't and afraid to ask anyone else, lest he should know. Can you imagine never knowing what time it was? Thank goodness for twilight!

(EMILY rises)

Father never kissed us good night in his life. I know he loved us, but oh, he was so — austere. Why, he hardly ever smiled!

(EMILY has gotten the picture of her father)

I remember the day we went to the photographer to have his picture taken.

(She shows it to the Audience*)*

That poor photographer, trying to be cordial and put Father at ease!

He said, "Er — Squire Dickinson. Could you smile a little? Please?"

Father said, "I am smiling!"

You see? He looks like a bear. He didn't approve of Santa Claus and all such prowling gentlemen.

Father was the only one in the house to say "damn." Someone in every family ought to say damn, of course. And when *he* said it, he meant it. Why, if his newspaper was ever misplaced — *Damn!* No one else was allowed to say it but Father. It was absolutely forbidden.

(She replaces the picture)

Father forbade many things. When my sister, Vinnie, was a girl, she enjoyed showing off her pretty white shoulders by wearing her summer frocks quite low . . .

(She demonstrates to the Audience*)*

. . . about here. It was the fashion. And then she'd languish about the house looking dreamy-eyed, primping in front of the mirror, running to the window every time a boy walked by the house.

(EMILY imitates her sister)

Hello, Benjamin!

Father could take only so much of this. Then he'd bark at her, "Lavinia! Don't be so affected! Put on a shawl!" And poor Vin would flounce dramatically out of the room and stomp up the steps to her room and slam the door. Bang! She pouted the rest of the day. Trouble was, she was even prettier when she pouted.

But Father was — oh, so proper. Very demanding. Inflexible. That's why any show of leniency or understanding on his part would disarm us completely. I remember when he discovered I was writing till two or three o'clock in the morning.

(She goes to the bedroom and sits at her desk, becoming absorbed in writing. Then she looks up, startled)

But Father — I thought you were asleep.

No, I didn't notice the time.

Two o'clock? Is it that late?

But this is the only time the house is quiet, Father. Except for Vinnie — she snores like a poker and shovel and pair of tongs.

Yes, Father. I know you have a rule about early rising. But I haven't missed one morning, have I?

Tired? I do?

Well, I was — writing.

Yes. Good night, Father.

(She turns back)

Just a — poem — Father.

Now?

Out loud?

(She clears her throat)

To make a prairie — a *prairie*, Father . . .

> To make a prairie it takes a clover and one bee,
> One clover, and a bee,
> And revery.
> The revery alone will do,
> If bees are few.

Another one? Yes, Father, I do.

(She stoops down beside the box of poems)

Excuse me. I keep my finished ones in here.

(EMILY removes a poem and sits at her desk again)

I'll tell you how the Sun rose —
A Ribbon at a time —
The Steeples swam in Amethyst —
The news, like Squirrels, ran —
The Hills untied their Bonnets —
The Bobolinks — begun —
Then I said softly to myself —
"That must have been the Sun"!
But how he set — I know not —
There seemed a purple stile
That little Yellow boys and girls
Were climbing all the while —
Till when they reached the other side,
A Dominie in Gray —
Put gently up the evening Bars —
And led the flock away —

Cancel the rule for me? Then I can sleep late in the morning. Oh, *thank you*, Father!

(To the AUDIENCE*)*

See what I mean?

(She replaces the poem in the box on the floor)

He sometimes yielded, when I least expected it. I'm sure he didn't know how obsessed I was with the desire for publication. In fact, I don't remember Father ever reading my poetry. He didn't seem to have an esthetic sense. I mean, he showed so little interest in anything but his law practice and the duties of being college treasurer. Like the night of Jenny Lind, the Swedish Nightingale. Father took us to the concert. The bouquets fell in showers, and she sang and sang and sang and sang. We got home after mid-night! Father sat all evening like old Abraham, looking mad. Well, her trills *were* a bit curious. We didn't care a fig for the Swedish Nightingale. We'd rather have heard a Yankee Whippoorwill. But I suspect what was on Father's mind was the four thousand dollars she was taking out of town!

Then, one autumn evening . . .

(The sky begins to glow with beautiful golds and oranges and reds)

. . . we were all startled by a violent church bell ringing, and thinking of nothing but fire — we rushed out in the street to see.

Vinnie! Mother! Quick!

(EMILY in shawl is now downstage)

The sky was a beautiful red, bordering on a crimson, and rays of a gold pink color were constantly shooting off from a kind of sun in the center.

People were alarmed at this phenomenon, supposing that fires somewhere were coloring the sky. But it was the northern lights, the aurora borealis! The exhibition lasted for nearly fifteen minutes, and the streets of Amherst were full of people, wondering and admiring.

And who do you think first noticed that remarkable sky?

Who do you imagine ran over to the church to ring the bells and call everyone's attention to such beauty?

My Father!

The first time we parted — eighteen forty-seven — I was sixteen. I graduated from Amherst Academy and entered Mount Holyoke Female Seminary, which was run by a *dragon*. Oh, I wanted to tell you about her! Mary Lyon ran the school — a noble lady, sometimes known as "The Dragon"! I liked Miss Lyon, even though she laid down strict rules for her girls. Unfortunately, her main concern was for our spiritual health.

We were classified in three categories. We were either "professed Christians" — that was Jane Gridley's group; we "had hope" — that was Olivia Coleman's group; or we were "without hope" — and naturally, I was in charge of *that* group. After Miss Lyon made a vigorous appeal for converts, the "without hopes" were reduced considerably. I'll never forget it. One evening we impenitent girls were invited by Miss Lyon to a meeting in Room B — "the dungeon." And we were told to bring the Bible.

(EMILY *walks slowly to the parlor*)

I told Olivia this would happen, that Miss Lyon would ask everyone who desired to be employed in service to Christ to rise at the meeting and declare herself.

Courage, Emily!

(*She curtsies*)

Good evening, Miss Lyon.

(She sits in the parlor chair)

I'm sorry, Miss Lyon, but I can't rise.

I know I'm the only one left without hope, but the spirit hasn't moved me yet.

Yes, Ma'am. I desire to be good.

Yes, I do want to please my parents, but I'm not yet persuaded to be a Christian.

Oh, I appreciate your offer of mercy, Ma'am, and I know the world is sinful and wicked, but the path of duty doesn't look — well, it doesn't look very attractive to me.

But I *have* read the Bible, Miss Lyon, Old *and* New Testaments.

Well, I thought at first it was an arid book. But then I found it wise and a bit — merry.

Merry. Yes, Ma'am.

M — E — R — R — Y.

(EMILY stands)

She did look like a dragon. I think it was the nose. But I mustn't laugh at Miss Lyon, for I believe she had a pure heart, and that is the important thing, isn't it?

> Perhaps the "Kingdom of Heaven's" changed —
> I hope the "Children" there

Won't be "new fashioned" when I come
And laugh at me — and stare —

I hope the Father in the skies
Will lift his little girl —
Old fashioned — naughty — everything —
Over the stile of "Pearl."

(She has stood and come downstage)

I didn't return to Holyoke the following year. You might
say — I wore out my welcome with Miss Lyon. And
Father wanted me home, besides. He said it was for my
health. But I think Father was lonely. Austin was soon to
leave for college, and Father couldn't bear to have the
family separated. More than one away at a time was too
much for him.

All the while Austin was at home, they'd do nothing but
fight. But the minute they were separated, they became
devoted friends. There was no one living for whom Father
had such respect, as for my brother, Austin.

Oh, but no one missed him more than I did.

(EMILY turns and calls offstage)

Austin! The coach is here!

(She goes downstage and opens an umbrella)

Each time he left, I stood out there in the road, watching
the stagecoach disappear. I'd wait for Austin to turn
around. I had to be sure he saw me. It was almost a su-

perstition with me. I thought that if he didn't see me as the stagecoach went behind the hill, that we'd never meet again. So it could be raining or snowing, but there I stood, waiting for his last look through that little window in the coach.

Those times seem far off now, a great way, as things we did when children. I wish we were children now, and the nails hung full of coats again, and the chairs hung full of hats, the umbrellas all in a row, and I could count the slippers under the kitchen chair. I wish we were *always* children. How to grow up, I don't know.

(She takes up sewing and sits in the parlor)

Just before my twenty-fifth birthday, Austin came home from law school, and he never left Amherst again. But I think he wanted to. When he graduated, he had an offer to go with a law firm in Chicago. He was about ready to leave, when Father offered to build him a house right next door if he'd stay.

It was the easy answer — in some ways. Not so easy in others.

But Father always got his way. And Austin stayed.

Probably Sue influenced him too. Susan Gilbert was engaged to marry Austin at the time Father made his generous . . .

(Mildly sarcastic)

. . . and unselfish offer.

From this room we can look over to Sue's house. We call it "The Evergreens." This, of course, is "The Homestead." There's a path between, just wide enough for two who love, but . . .

(Sadly)

. . . no one uses it much anymore. Sue and I used it more than anyone. Sue was the only one who understood my need to write. I loved her dearly. But she didn't understand my love. Perhaps I don't understand it myself.

I've always been intense about relationships. At times, my love overwhelms people. And it puzzles me. My business is to love. It's dangerous to love as I do. Bliss is so unnatural, don't you think?

The path is overgrown with weeds now.

I guess it's best to abandon paths when you find they lead nowhere.

(EMILY looks around the room, remembering)

In this parlor we always met for morning prayers, as far back as childhood. Everyone in the family was religious, except me, and they addressed an Eclipse every morning whom they called, "Our Father."

(She stands and puts on her bonnet)

I can still hear Father say in a most militant way, *"I say unto you."* It always gave me a chill.

Why is religion made so grim? So dull! Why should we be made to feel so guilty? Sermons, sermons, sermons! I only heard one sermon that I really liked. And that was when the Reverend Dwight preached on unbelief.

Sermons on unbelief always did attract me.

It was on a sweltering July Sabbath that I decided to stop attending church altogether. Well, I was old enough to make that decision. I was almost thirty. I came home very hot and faded, having witnessed a couple of baptisms, three admissions to church, a Supper of the Lord, and some other minor transactions — including the sermon, wheezed by Reverend Leland: "Make a joyful noise [wheeze] unto the Lord, all ye lands [wheeze], and come before his presence with singing [wheeze]."

Singing, indeed!

Poor Reverend Leland!

(She removes her bonnet)

> Some keep the Sabbath going to Church —
> I keep it, staying at Home —
> With a Bobolink for a Chorister —
> And an Orchard, for a Dome —
>
> Some keep the Sabbath in Surplice —
> I just wear my Wings —

And instead of tolling the Bell, for Church,
Our little Sexton — sings.

God preaches, a noted Clergyman —
And the sermon is never long,
So instead of getting to Heaven, at last —
I'm going, all along.

In the name of the Bee —
And of the Butterfly —
And of the Breeze — Amen!

Oh, you agree with me?

When the family went to church, I was never alone. God
was sitting right there — looking into my very soul.

(EMILY *hangs up her bonnet and picks up a newspaper.
She then sits in the parlor*)

How do you spend your evenings? Vinnie and I read the
Springfield *Republican* every night. I read the news aloud
while she sews. Vinnie has an odd liking for those stories
of accidents where trains meet each other unexpectedly, or
gentlemen in factories get their heads cut off quite infor-
mally. The author relates them in such a sprightly way,
Vinnie finds the stories quite attractive. She was disappointed last night that there weren't more accidents.

Oh, here's one you'll love, Vinnie! "TRAIN HITS
WOMAN ON MILL RIVER TRESTLE."

"Cornelia Snell, fifty-four" — Snell! — "was killed last
Wednesday by the Belchertown Express as she struggled
vainly to free her foot from a railroad switch." Her foot,

Vinnie! "Engineer Grover W. Putnam declared, 'By the time I saw the poor lady and her dog, it was too late.'"

Yes, Vinnie. "She leaves her husband, Noah L. Snell, and eight children." Eight little Snells. Oh, the dog survived! It jumped clear!

No, Vinnie, the casket was closed! She was hit by a *train!* Services were held already, it says — "last Friday" — Hambley and Son in Springfield. Some sixty attended.

Her children are planting an evergreen in her memory near the spot. Isn't that sweet, Vinnie?

(Long pause)

I wonder why she didn't take off her shoe?

Oh, I suppose she tried. But trains are so fast these days.

Vinnie — Vin — oh, she's asleep.

(To the AUDIENCE*)*

Speaking of trains, there wasn't a more exciting day in Amherst than the day of the Railroad Decision in eighteen fifty-two. It made all the headlines.

*(*EMILY *stands)*

Father was really satisfied with himself. He had fought for the railroad to come into Amherst. It seemed like a fairy tale, a most miraculous event in our lives. The day the train finally arrived was called New London Day. It was hot and dusty, but nobody cared for that. Father was, as

usual, Chief Marshal of the day. He went marching around
the town like Mr. Amherst himself, with New London at
his heels — like some old Roman general on a Triumph
Day.

I sat out there in Professor Tyler's woods and saw the train
move off.

> I like to see it lap the Miles —
> And lick the Valleys up —
> And stop to feed itself at Tanks —
> And then — prodigious step
>
> Around a Pile of Mountains —
> And supercilious peer
> In Shanties — by the sides of Roads —
> And then a Quarry pare
>
> To fit its sides
> And crawl between
> Complaining all the while
> In horrid — hooting stanza —
> Then chase itself down Hill —
>
> And neigh like Boanerges —
> Then — punctual as a Star
> Stop — docile and omnipotent
> At its own stable door —

It's fall. And you know what New England autumns are
like. Amherst has gone to Eden, and the moon rides like
a girl through a topaz town. Well, Vinnie says that autumn is "one long chore." Can you imagine? She's out
there now, picking apples for cider.

Oh! The ladder!

(EMILY runs to the window)

Vinnie! Be careful on that ladder! It's broken!

(To the AUDIENCE)

Vinnie's always falling off of something. But she's practical. She knows where everything is in this house, from a lost quotation to last year's muffler.

Vinnie wears white cotton stockings, even though everyone else is wearing black. She thinks her feet will be poisoned by the dye in the black stockings.

(EMILY chases the cat with a newspaper)

Buffy! Buffy, you one-eyed monster! Leave my yarn alone! Buffy!

Vinnie's one big passion is cats. Unfortunately, mine is birds. And now she has a *new* cat — Drummy-doodles! It catches a mouse an hour. We call it the minute hand.

Look at that! Feathers all over the orchard! They're floating everywhere!

Vinnie! Vinnie! Your cats are killing my birds!

Blame the Creator? Blame your cats! I warn you — I'm going to find assassins for them!

(She has let off steam. Now she addresses the AUDIENCE*)*

Vinnie thinks her cats are a little lower than the angels. A china saucer for each one. Indeed! If she had her way, they'd dine on sherry and hummingbird cutlets every night.

It's so weird and so vastly mysterious. Vinnie sleeps by my side. Her care is in some sort motherly. But if we had come up for the first time from two wells where we had been bred, her astonishment wouldn't be greater at some things I say.

Like Father was.

Mother was different. Mother didn't care for thought. Consequently, she never listened to what I said.

We all lived together like friendly and absolute monarchs here at Homestead, each in his own domain. Yet . . .

(She slowly walks into her bedroom)

I was the slightest in the House —
I took the smallest Room —
At night, my little Lamp, and Book —
And one Geranium —

So stationed I could catch the Mint
That never ceased to fall —
And just my Basket —
Let me think — I'm sure
That this was all —

I never spoke — unless addressed —
And then, 'twas brief and low —

I could not bear to live — aloud —
The Racket shamed me so —

And if it had not been so far —
And any one I knew
Were going — I had often thought
How noteless — I could die —

(EMILY *is at her desk, a magazine in hand*)

Do you read *The Atlantic Monthly?*

Well, in the April issue, eighteen sixty-two — an article
appeared, inviting young writers to submit their work . . .

(Reading)

"Charge your style with life," said the author, Thomas
Wentworth Higginson.

This was what I was waiting for! Sue agreed. We spent
days trying to find just the right poems to send. But Sue
thought Father would disapprove.

(EMILY *is crumpling papers as she discards one sheet
after another*)

No, he'll approve soon enough, when my poems bring
honor to his name.

Now, find one that's a good contrast to the other three,
and I'll finish this letter.

But the letter is important too. It has to attract his attention. I want him to see that I'm *different*. Not just a country poetess sending little verses to the city editor — but really inspired! He says right here, "Every editor is always hungering and thirsting after a genius."

(Working as she talks)

No, Sue, not that one.

That's closer. But not quite.

Sue. See how you like this . . .

(She reads her letter aloud)

"Mr. Higginson,

"Are you too deeply occupied to say if my Verse is Alive? The Mind is so near itself — it cannot see, distinctly — and I have none to ask — Should you think it breathed — and had you the leisure to tell me, I should feel quick gratitude —

"If I make the mistake — that you dared to tell me — would give me sincerer honor — toward you — I enclose my name — asking you, if you please — Sir — to tell me what is true? That you will not betray me — it is needless to ask — since Honor is its own pawn."

Well?

No, I'm not going to sign it. Isn't that humble of me?

Oh, of course. But on a little card slipped into the poems.

(She produces the card and signs it)

Well, he'll find it. He'll look for it.

"Emily Dickinson" — no . . .

"*E*. Dickinson." Mysterious?

(She shows it to SUE*)*

It *is* provocative, isn't it? Ought to whet his curiosity, I'd say. And then, when he reads my poems, won't he go wild? Do you think I should send more than four poems? How about six? Or ten?

*(*EMILY *is now on the floor, rummaging through the box of poems)*

No, not that one, Sue. How about . . .

> I taste a liquor never brewed —
> From Tankards scooped in Pearl —
> Not all the Vats upon the Rhine
> Yield such an Alcohol!
>
> Inebriate of Air — am I —
> And Debauchee of Dew —
> Reeling — thro endless summer days —
> From inns of Molten Blue —
>
> When "Landlords" turn the drunken Bee
> Out of the Foxglove's door —

When Butterflies — renounce their "drams" —
I shall but drink the more!

Till Seraphs swing their snowy Hats —
And Saints — to windows run —
To see the little Tippler
Leaning against the — Sun —

Oh, I know, Sue. You're right. Too giddy. But I love it.

How about . . .

       The Pedigree of Honey
       Does not concern the Bee —
       A Clover, any time, to him,
       Is Aristocracy —

No?

       A Bird came down the Walk —
       He did not know I saw —
       He bit an Angleworm in halves
       And ate the fellow, raw.

No. No bird poems, Sue.

(She mulls over several)

Wait! I have it! "Safe in their Alabaster Chambers."

Safe in their Alabaster Chambers —
Untouched by Morning
And untouched by Noon —
Sleep the meek members of the Resurrection —

Rafter of satin,
And Roof of stone.

Light laughs the breeze
In her Castle of sunshine —
Babbles the Bee in a stolid Ear,
Pipe the Sweet Birds in ignorant cadence —
Ah, what sagacity perished here!

Grand go the Years — in the Crescent — above them —
Worlds scoop their Arcs —
And Firmaments — row —
Diadems — drop — and Doges — surrender —
Soundless as dots — on a Disc of Snow —

That's the fourth!

(Excited, she sits at her desk and writes)

"Mr. Thomas Wentworth Higginson, *Atlantic Monthly*, Washington and School Streets, Boston, Massachusetts."

Oh, now we must throw away these scraps of paper!

No one must know that the famous and mysterious "E. Dickinson" writes second and third drafts of her letters!

Oh, look how long I've kept you! Austin will be waiting for dinner. Thank you, my darling. And I'll let you know the minute I hear.

(She waves to SUE. *After a pause,* EMILY *addresses the* AUDIENCE*)*

Professor Higginson answered my letter, but not in the way I had hoped. I thanked him for the surgery. It wasn't as painful as I supposed. He did ask to see more poems. And I sent them. I wrote him often — even began calling him my Preceptor, and myself his Scholar. Eight years of correspondence! Eight years of putting my hopes on the shelf. And then, when I was forty, the incredible happened. *Thomas Wentworth Higginson was coming to Amherst.*

(EMILY *rises with a letter in hand*)

Face to face at last! Now — *now* we can accomplish something!

(*She reads* HIGGINSON'S *letter as she stands center stage*)

"I look forward to meeting with you, and will come directly from my visit with President Stearns at the College." He says, "The fifteenth."

(*She curtsies*)

Oh, dear Friend! I will be at home, and *glad.*

I — I've been so afraid. It's like being terrified of midnight when I was a child. But *now* . . .

> It's time to smooth the Hair —
> And get the Dimples ready —
> And wonder we could care
> For that old — faded Midnight —
> That frightened — but an Hour!

He's coming to Amherst at last!

It seems *I'm going to be famous!*

(EMILY *calls to* SUE *as she runs off stage left*)

Sue! Sue! I've got the most glorious news! Wait till you hear! He's coming! He's coming!

Act Two

～～～～

The stage is the same. The ensuing scene is a continuation of the conclusion of Act One.

EMILY *runs in from stage left and goes directly to her bedroom.*

EMILY

Maggie! Watch for the coach. I'll be upstairs.

(She moves downstage, where she briefly sews together a booklet of poems as she talks)

Oh, surely, *this is the day.*

(Shouting downstairs to MAGGIE*)*

Maggie! When he comes, ask him to wait in the hall.

(She looks at her watch)

Oh, it's almost time. I wonder how long he'll stay? Oh — what to say?

(Practicing her introduction)

Oh, Mr. Higginson. How is *dear* Mrs. Higginson? Good noon, Professor Higginson. How is Mrs. Higginson?

(She picks up a fan)

Enchanted, Mr. Higginson. How is sweet Mrs. Higginson?
. . . Another confinement? . . . Sherry? It's Father's best
. . . Yes, August *is* a glorious month.

(She gestures to a chair)

Please.

(Much laughter and fanning)

Oh, Mr. Higginson! How droll! I wish I'd thought of
that. Oh, how witty! . . . My favorite books? Oh, let me
see. *Jane Eyre* I loved. And *The Mill on the Floss.* And
of course — *your* inspired novel . . .

(She produces the book from her desk drawer)

. . . *Malbone.* How *did* you do it? . . . Oh, Shakespeare
is my lexicon. I owe *that* to Tutor Crowell. He made us
read *everything.* He was . . .

(She hears the coach)

Oh, a coach.

(She runs to the window)

It's stopping — oh, he's taller than I thought. And so im-
posing. Maggie! The door!

(EMILY runs to her desk, puts on her shawl. She then makes

*several attempts to select poems to take downstairs with her,
finally deciding upon the box of poems itself)*

Courage, Emily.

(She goes to the parlor)

Mr. Higginson.

(Breathless and tense)

And *I* to meet *you.* Uh, how long are you going to stay?
Oh, what I mean is — why has it taken eight years? Oh,
I know you've been so busy. And then, you *were* away in
the — the war — the *Civil* War, wasn't it?

War to me is so — oblique. I can't grasp it. *My* wars are
laid away in books.

*(She sits on the low chest, very excited. Her mind is run-
ning on one track only — publication)*

But now, to the real purpose of your visit! I've been waiting to hear from your own lips — what you are planning
for my poems. I have them right here — all the ones I've
sent you.

(She has them at hand)

These are the first four. And here . . .

*(EMILY shuffles through many more papers, spilling some
on the floor and scrambling to pick them up)*

. . . are the later ones. I've bound them together. Oh, *this* one . . .

I'll tell you how the Sun rose . . .

. . . *this* was Sue's choice. Sue is my sister-in-law. That's her house over there. It wasn't what I would have chosen. But perhaps for publication, it's more appropriate — more appealing to the reading public.

(Her words tumble over each other)

But you will be the best judge of that, Mr. Higginson. Now, I have many more that you might feel would be better in a printed collection. Many, oh — well over a thousand you've never even read! Enough for several volumes, I should think. Oh, and I would prefer morocco-bound.

(She looks for his reaction)

Oh, dear, I must apologize, Mr. Higginson. I'm not giving you a chance to say anything. But could you tell me how to grow, or is it unconveyed, like melody or witchcraft?

Well — no matter — please feel free to choose the poems you think are best for a book. And as for publishers, I'll rely solely upon your judgment. After all, you *are* my Preceptor.

(EMILY finally sits back. Then slowly, she leans forward. What she is hearing from HIGGINSON is shocking. Her mouth falls open)

But . . .

(She clutches the arms of the chair)

But — my meter is new — experimental. Not spasmodic!

Bad rhymes? Oh, no. You don't understand what I'm try-ing to — if I could only explain . . .

Uncontrolled? But, Mr. Higginson, when I try to orga-nize, my little force explodes.

(She picks up a handful of poems)

But surely a publisher will recognize . . .

(EMILY stops, her hand in midair. She is crushed)

Surely . . .

(To the AUDIENCE)

A great Hope fell
You heard no noise
The Ruin was within
Oh cunning wreck that told no tale
And let no Witness in

A not admitting of the wound
Until it grew so wide
That all my Life had entered it
And there were troughs beside

A closing of the simple lid
That opened to the sun

Until the tender Carpenter
Perpetual nail it down —

(She walks to the bedroom)

I still send him poems. But always — from his polite re-
plies, I get the uneasy feeling that they end up in some
dusty drawer in his office.

(She reclines on the bed)

I can talk about this now. But oh, when I heard Mr. Higginson's words — I became ill.

I understand another poet met with the same disappointing
reception from Mr. Higginson. But *he* didn't give up as I
did. Here . . .

(She holds up a book)

. . . he got his poems published somehow. And his book
has gone through nine editions already. Mr. Higginson
says his poems are absolutely scandalous! His name? —
(pause) — Walt Whitman!

> Success is counted sweetest
> By those who ne'er succeed.
> To comprehend a nectar
> Requires sorest need.
>
> Not one of all the purple Host
> Who took the Flag today
> Can tell the definition
> So clear of Victory

As he defeated — dying —
On whose forbidden ear
The distant strains of triumph
Burst agonized and clear!

Perhaps no one will ever read my poems. They seem to me like an undelivered letter lost in transit. Destiny is strange.

(Under her breath, deriding herself)

Going to be famous!

If fame belonged to me, I couldn't escape her. If she didn't, the longest day would pass me on the chase, and the approbation of my dog would forsake me, then. My barefoot rank is better.

We never know how high we are
Till we are asked to rise
And then if we are true to plan
Our statures touch the skies —

(EMILY has risen from the bed and gone to her writing desk. She has removed her shawl)

But do you know who came to see me recently?

Helen Jackson, the writer. Facts, not phosphorescence. Remember? She brought me a lovely selection of columbine seeds from Colorado. And of all things, she's after me to publish. At *this* late date. She says she'll assume full charge. Helen could do it. She's very influential. And — aggressive. Helen of Troy will die, but Helen of Colorado, never!

(She sits at the desk)

But I said, "My meridian has passed." I told Helen that, to me, publication is the auction of the mind of man. I've reached that conclusion, and I'm at peace with it.

(She comes downstage)

Like the warbler that I found on a bush at the foot of the garden.

"Why sing," I said, "since nobody hears?"

(With exaltation)

"My business is to sing!" And away it rose.

My business is to sing! What difference does it make if no one listens? Perhaps you laugh at me! Perhaps the whole United States are laughing at me too! I can't stop for that! Just to have been made alive is so chief a thing, all else inevitably adds. I find ecstasy in living. The mere sense of living is joy enough. Take all away from me, but leave me ecstasy!

(EMILY kneels on a blanket downstage to plant seeds)

Egotism is a hard thing to deal with. When I wanted fame, it seemed — selfish. But Helen says my *current* attitude is selfish. Which direction to take, I don't know. What do *you* think?

(Facetiously)

It's not that I haven't *had* fame, of sorts.

(Her eyes twinkle)

One October, my rye and Indian bread won second prize at the Cattle Show. Second prize was seventy-five cents. And in case you missed the newspaper, my heliotropes won honorable mention.

> I'm Nobody! Who are you?
> Are you — Nobody — Too?
> Then there's a pair of us?
> Don't tell! They'd banish us — you know.

(Forthright)

> How dreary — to be — Somebody!
> How public — like a Frog —
> To tell your name — the livelong day —
> To an admiring Bog!

Vinnie always said that my withdrawal into seclusion was only "a happen." I suppose my not marrying was only a happen too. Vin received an offer of marriage — once. Oh, yes, she did.

But it came to nothing. Contrary to town gossip, she wanted very much to marry Joseph Lyman. But he fell in love with Laura Baker. She was that pretty girl in yellow. You remember.

And that was that.

Vinnie did *not* give up marriage to remain with me!

Don't you listen to that Henny Sweetser.

Vin never speaks of marriage anymore. But I think she lives much of the time in the State of Regret.

My Country is Truth!

I don't regret my aloneness. I accept the pattern of life as it came to me — or as I caused it to be. I'd have let Vinnie go. But she'd *never* let *me* go. No, in her mind, my presence justifies the day-to-day boredom of her life. I think it has even become a kind of martyrdom.

(EMILY *becomes animated*)

One summer day — I was here in the garden with my Canterbury bells — a man who secretly loved me came to Amherst *to take me away*.

Father and Mother were gone for the afternoon, and Vinnie was terrified at the thought of losing me. She became hysterical. I could hear her screaming at him all the way out here.

(*She runs into the parlor*)

Vinnie! Vinnie! Get control of yourself!

He's in Father's library?

But I didn't know he was coming!

No. No. We had no such plans. Believe me, I would have told you.

He said that? He wants me to leave with him? Today?
Now?

I don't know! I have to think! Please — so I'm forty-two!
Does that make me foolish?

Vinnie? Stop screaming! He'll hear! Look at me. I love
you. I love Father and Mother. I don't want to hurt anyone. But I've got to decide this myself.

Vinnie! Where are you going? Come back!

(To the AUDIENCE*)*

She ran like a raving lunatic over to The Evergreens and
came back dragging Sue. By the time they came hurtling
through the kitchen door, my friend was gone. I sent him
away.

I can't tell you his name. Forgive me. He was married.

(She puts on her apron)

But I'll never get over Vinnie. She acted as if it were the
end of the world. And even though she was sorry for the
things she said — do you know, she turned right around
and did the same thing last year, when Judge Otis P. Lord
proposed to me? Just because he was eighteen years older
than I, Vinnie once again went absolutely mad.

(She sits and begins darning a white stocking)

Of course, she changed her tune when he died in March.

Why she is so self-righteous, I'll never know. Austin is having an affair right now with — oh, I shouldn't tell you this — well, he *is!* With Professor Todd's wife, Mabel; and Vinnie doesn't object to *that* at all. In fact, she carries messages between them in her sewing basket. She acts like a middle-aged Cupid.

But it was Judge Lord's niece, Abby Farley, who had the most to say. She was disgusted by our courtship. After the Judge died, she called me a little hussy with loose morals — said I'm crazy about men, and insane besides.

Even one of those is bad enough. But all three?

Abby looks a little tart, but Otis said she makes excellent apple pies. I guess she knows that Otis was paying me attention while his wife was still alive.

(She leans forward to the Audience*)*

Does that shock you?

(Quietly)

Oh, I know I'm plain — and small, like the wren. But my hair is bold, like the chestnut burr. And my eyes, like the sherry in the glass that the guest leaves. I never had but one picture taken of myself — when I was seventeen.

(She points to the pictures on the piano)

It's not among those.

(She opens a drawer to get the picture)

This daguerreotype.

(She takes it downstage and shows it to the Audience*)*

Plain. Now there's a word *not* to lift your hat to. That's Vinnie's touch, the neck ribbon. She made it.

I know what people say. "Poor Emily — the only kangaroo among the beauties." Is it any wonder I keep it in a drawer?

(She puts it back)

But I'll have you know, plain or not, I had more than one suitor. And they were all married. And older than I.

But there was really only one.

(She sits again)

Only one.

It was in Philadelphia years ago that I first saw Charles Wadsworth. I was twenty-four. I hadn't planned to tell you this. Vinnie and I had visited Father in Washington while he was a congressman. On the way home, we stayed two weeks with the Colemans in Philadelphia. We attended the Presbyterian church where Mr. Wadsworth was minister.

When I first laid eyes on him that Sunday morning . . .

(EMILY now seems transfigured)

. . . it was as if heaven's own lightning struck me. Here before me was a Christlike man. He seemed like — Gabriel standing before the congregation.

When I walked out of the church into the brilliant morning . . .

(EMILY is now in a state of ecstasy)

. . . the light in my heart was shining even brighter. His voice haunted me. I couldn't shake off the enchantment, even after I returned to Amherst.

I wrote to him, at first hesitant. A cautious letter, asking about spiritual things — redemption, immortality. And finally, in his answers, I detected a response not unlike my own emotions. But more subtle, sensitive, hidden.

It's an exquisite experience to love someone in a bodiless way, like fleshless lovers, forever one. Such love was the limit of my dream, the focus of my prayer. It made me different from before, as if I breathed superior air. Oh —

> Wild Nights — Wild Nights!
> Were I with thee
> Wild Nights should be
> Our luxury!
>
> Futile — the Winds —
> To a Heart in port —
> Done with the Compass —
> Done with the Chart!

Rowing in Eden —
Ah, the Sea!
Might I but moor — Tonight —
In Thee!

(She has removed her apron)

I called him my Master. I spoke with him only twice in
my life — twenty years apart, the first time, in eighteen
sixty. He came to me again, three years ago.

Vinnie came running to get me. She said, "The gentleman
with the deep voice wants to see you, Emily."

Again — his voice is at the door —
I feel the old *Degree* —
I hear him ask the servant
For such an one — as me —

*(EMILY takes a flower from a vase and she walks slowly to
center stage)*

I take a *flower* — as I go —
My face to *justify* —
He never *saw* me — *in this life* —
I might *surprise* his eye!

I cross the Hall with *mingled* steps —
I — silent — pass the door —
I look on all this world *contains* —
Just his face — nothing more!

*(EMILY steps forward. She is struggling with emotion as
she converses)*

Where did you come from?

Ah, the pulpit to the train. But why didn't you tell me you were coming, so I could have it to hope for?

Oh, then you didn't know yourself. You just came.

How long was your journey?

Twenty years! Yes, it has been that long, hasn't it?

But I'm older too — Master. But the love is the same.

Oh, no, say I may wait for you. I waited a long time, Master. But I can wait more.

Till my hazel hair is dappled — and you carry the cane. Then I can look at my watch, and if the day is too far declined, we can take the chances for heaven!

(She kneels)

Master — open your life wide and take me in forever.

And I will be your best little girl. Nobody else will see me but you. But that's enough. I shall not want any more.

Forgive me. I know . . .

> I cannot live with You —
> It would be Life —
> And Life is over there —
> Behind the Shelf

The Sexton keeps the Key to —
Putting up
Our Life — His Porcelain —
Like a Cup —

Discarded of the Housewife —

So We must keep apart —
You there — I — here —
With just the Door ajar
That Oceans are — and Prayer —
And that Pale Sustenance —
Despair.

Thank you. And I am so moved just to look in your face while you look in mine.

(She is now standing)

Will you come to Amherst again?

You can't?

I understand.

Yes, I'm content. I shall always be content — now.

Goodbye . . . Master.

(She sits in the parlor chair and addresses the AUDIENCE*)*

It's easier to look behind at a pain than to see it coming. When the best is gone, I know that other things are not of consequence. The heart wants what it wants, or else it doesn't care.

Last year, in April — my Master died.

> Will there really be a "Morning"?
> Is there such a thing as "Day"?
> Could I see it from the mountains
> If I were as tall as they?
>
> Has it feet like Water lilies?
> Has it feathers like a Bird?
> Is it brought from famous countries
> Of which I have never heard?

(She stands)

> Oh some Scholar! Oh some Sailor!
> Oh some Wise Man from the skies!
> Please to tell a little Pilgrim
> Where the place called "Morning" lies!

(EMILY puts on a cloak)

Yes, I still write poetry, but not as much as I used to. There are so few listeners, and those who should be the best listeners — like Professor Higginson — are deaf.

But even yet . . .

(She goes downstage)

. . . when I see a tall pale snowstorm stalking through the fields and bowing at my window, I find I must translate my feeling into poetry.

I sometimes put both hands on the windowpane and try to think how birds fly, and imitate, and fail. I could make a balloon of a dandelion, but the fields are gone. I talk of all these things with my dog, and his eyes grow meaning, and his shaggy feet keep a slower pace. Animals have a natural, simple wisdom. Except chickens, of course! At present we have twenty-four invalid hens, who do nothing so vulgar as lay an egg.

But I do remember one Christmas morning, the hens came to the door with Santa Claus, and the cats washed themselves in the open air without chilling their tongues. Atmospherically, it was the most beautiful Christmas on record. Maggie gave her hens a check for potatoes, and each of the cats a gilt-edged bone — and the horses had both new blankets from Boston. It was a lovely Christmas!

Vinnie's cats leave the chickens alone. They're good about that. But in summer they're forever catching snakes and carrying them into the kitchen. Poor Vinnie is deathly afraid of snakes. When I hear a scream and a crash from the kitchen, I know what's happened.

When we were little, I'd hide behind a tree with a garter snake in my hand — and when Vinnie came along, I'd wave it in her face and chase her all over the orchard.

Well, Austin did it too.

I love those little green ones — you know the ones I mean? — that slide around by your shoes in the grass, and make it rustle with their elbows!

> A narrow Fellow in the Grass
> Occasionally rides —

You may have met Him — did you not
His notice sudden is —

The Grass divides as with a Comb —
A spotted shaft is seen —
And then it closes at your feet
And opens further on —

He likes a Boggy Acre
A Floor too cool for Corn —
Yet when a Boy, and Barefoot —
I more than once at Noon
Have passed, I thought, a Whip lash
Unbraiding in the Sun
When stooping to secure it
It wrinkled, and was gone —

Several of Nature's People
I know, and they know me —
I feel for them a transport
Of cordiality —

But never met this Fellow
Attended, or alone
Without a tighter breathing
And Zero at the Bone —

Did I tell you that my father loved animals? Well, he did.
He had beautiful horses.

(She removes her cloak and hangs it up)

During his last winter nine years ago, there were several
snowstorms, and the birds were so frightened and cold, they
sat by the kitchen door. Father went to the barn in his

slippers and came back with a breakfast of grain for each, and hid himself while he scattered it, lest it embarrass them. Ignorant of the name or fate of their benefactor, their descendants are singing this afternoon.

(EMILY *sits in the parlor chair*)

The last afternoon that my father lived, though with no premonition — I preferred to be with him, and invented an absence for Mother, Vinnie being asleep. He seemed peculiarly pleased, as I oftenest stayed with myself, and remarked as the afternoon withdrew, he "would like it not to end."

His pleasure almost embarrassed me, and my brother coming, I suggested they walk. Next morning I woke him for the train — and saw him no more.

We were eating our supper the fifteenth of June and Austin came in. He had a dispatch in his hand, and I saw by his face we were all lost, though I didn't know how. He said that Father was very sick, and he and Vinnie must go. The train had already gone. While horses were dressing — news came he was dead.

Father doesn't live with us now. He lives in a new house. Though it was built in an hour, it is better than this. He hasn't any garden, because he moved after gardens were made. So we take him the best flowers. And if we only knew *he* knew, perhaps we could stop crying. Though it is many nights, my mind never comes home.

At the funeral, Austin leaned over the coffin and kissed

Father's forehead and said, "There, Father. I never dared do that while you were living."

(She is overcome with emotion)

Excuse me.

(She rises and gestures to the window)

The birds that Father rescued are trifling in his trees. How flippant are the saved! They were even frolicking at the grave when Vinnie went there yesterday. Nature must be too young to feel, or many years too old.

I dream about Father every night, always a different dream, and forget what I'm doing daytimes — wondering *where he is.*

Without any body, I keep thinking. What kind can that be?

(She is now downstage)

You know, he never really learned how to play, and the straightest engine has its leaning hour.

His heart was pure and terrible, and I think no other like it exists. I'm glad there is immortality, but would have tested it myself, before entrusting him. Home is so far from home, since my father died.

> My life closed twice before its close —
> It yet remains to see
> If Immortality unveil
> A third event to me

So huge, so hopeless to conceive
As these that twice befell.
Parting is all we know of heaven,
And all we need of hell.

(She sits again in the parlor)

I shall always remember Father's coming home for noon-time dinner. Up Main Street he'd come, like a deacon, carrying his gold-headed cane and wearing his glossy beaver hat.

(EMILY springs to life)

Vinnie! Father's coming! Quick! Hide the mop and bucket!

Fell down the stairs? How did you . . .

Mother — take the handkerchief off your head.

What is that smell? Maggie! The cabbage! I think it's boiling over!

Vinnie, do something about Buffy. She's clawing the sofa!

Father's turning in the walk now! He's almost here! Mother, check the thermometer! I hung it in the east window! I'll see to the fire!

(Now yelling)

Buffy, get out of Father's chair at once! Scat!

(She swats at the cat with the newspaper)

What did you do with Father's newspaper, Vinnie?

No, it's *not* by his chair. I can't find it!

No, I didn't. I haven't even seen it yet. Oh, damn! Where is it?

(She realizes she is holding it)

I found it! It was — in your sewing basket!

Oh, there he is!

Sh! He's at the door.

(She runs to the entry and poses calmly)

Good noon, Father.

Did you have a fine morning at the office?

Oh, I'm sorry, Father.

Oh, very quiet here. A peaceful, restful morning. Wasn't it, Mother?

Vinnie? Limping? I hadn't noticed.

Awful smell? I don't smell anything.

The temperature?

Mother, what is the temperature? Father wants to know the temperature.

Fourteen? It's fourteen degrees, Father.

Your spectacles? You're wearing them, Father.

Your newspaper? Oh, I have it, Father. It's right here.

Wrinkled? Well, speak to Vinnie. It's Buffy's fault!

Maggie says it's ready. Your favorite, Father. Corned beef and cats — *cabbage!*

(To the AUDIENCE*)*

Pandemonium. Now the house is so quiet — with just Vinnie and me.

Since Father's death, I've worried about Vinnie. She says the strangest things. She treats me as if I were a child and she my nursemaid.

(She goes to the bedroom)

We had a terrible fire in Amherst on the Fourth of July, at night — and Vinnie tried to make me believe it was only the holiday fireworks!

She kept saying, "Emily, it's only the Fourth of July!" Well, I know a fire when I see one! And what a night that was for Mr. Frink and his noble fire brigade! It was lighter than day for a while. People running up and down Main

Street, shouting. It was like a *theater night in London.*
And Mother slept through it all. Vinnie's "only the Fourth
of July" — I shall always remember. I think she'll tell me
that when I die, to keep me from being afraid!

(EMILY *sits at her desk*)

A year after Father died, Mother had a stroke, in her room.
She never walked again.

I suspect Mother was afraid of dying. She always avoided
talking about it. One night, Austin and I were talking about
the extension of consciousness after death, and Mother told
Vinnie afterward — she thought it was "very improper."

Mother's dying almost stunned my spirit. She slipped from
our fingers like a flake gathered by the wind, and is now
part of the drift called "the infinite" . . .

. . . this was the way she died.

> And when her breath was done
> Took up her simple wardrobe
> And started for the sun.
> Her little figure at the gate
> The Angels must have spied,
> Since I could never find her
> Upon the mortal side.

You see, we were never intimate, as mother and children,
while she was our mother. But mines in the same ground
meet by tunneling, and when she became our child, the
affection came. Hold your parents tenderly, for the world
will seem a strange and lonely place when they're gone.

(EMILY's vitality springs back, like one who is tired of serious subjects)

Oh, I wish I were just a — blade of grass! Then all these problems of the dust wouldn't terrify me. Why do we cling to the body, to this little frame? Why are we afraid to let go? Or sad when others do? If my own machinery should get slightly out of gear . . .

(Imploringly)

. . . please! Someone stop the wheel! For I know that with belts and bands of gold, I shall whiz triumphant on the new streams!

> "Hope" is the thing with feathers —
> That perches in the soul —
> And sings the tune without the words —
> And never stops — at all —
>
> And sweetest — in the Gale — is heard —
> And sore must be the storm —
> That could abash the little Bird
> That kept so many warm —
>
> I've heard it in the chillest land —
> And on the strangest Sea —
> Yet, never, in Extremity,
> It asked a crumb — of Me.

(Pause)

I just heard from Helen. She's in California now. A seaside village called Santa Monica. Helen says the sun shines there all the time, and there is Bougainvillea everywhere.

And Abby Bliss and her husband have just founded the Syrian Protestant College in Beirut.

I've just had a lovely letter from Samuel Bowles and his wife, Mary. They're in Europe now, Paris, and they enclosed these stereopticon pictures.

(She holds up the viewer)

Isn't this a lovely thing?

(She looks into it)

The Scottish moors!

Vinnie gave it to me last Christmas. They're all the rage.

(She inserts another card)

Oh, this is the "Mona Lisa."

(A long pause as she looks)

I don't see what all the excitement is about.

(Another card)

This one is the Blue Grotto at Capri. Mary wrote they had to row out from the island to see it.

(She continues looking at cards in the viewer)

Everyone is somewhere, but Emily. Emily is here. *Always here.*

I never saw a Moor —
I never saw the Sea —
Yet know I how the Heather looks
And what a — Billow — no, wave —
And what a wave must be.

(She puts down the viewer and begins writing)

I never spoke with God
Nor visited in Heaven —
Yet certain am I of the spot
As if the Chart were given —

Vinnie says a little boy ran away from Amherst a few days ago. When asked where he was going, he replied, "Vermont or Asia."

What a smart little boy. I told Vinnie I wanted to run away too.

I think I frightened her.

(EMILY rises and goes to the parlor)

I sit here with my little whip, cracking the time away. I rise, because the sun shines and sleep is over with. And I brush my hair, and dress myself, and wonder what I am and who has made me so.

I tie my Hat — I crease my Shawl —
Life's little duties do — precisely —
As the very least
Were infinite — to me —

I put new Blossoms in the Glass
And throw the old — away —
I push a petal from my Gown
That anchored there — I weigh
The time 'twill be till six o'clock
I have so much to do —
And yet — Existence — some way back —
Stopped — struck — My ticking — through —
Therefore — we do life's labor —
Though life's Reward — be done —
With scrupulous exactness —
To hold our Senses — on —

(She sits in the parlor)

But there *are* the children. Thank God for that! They
keep my imagination keen and alive. Austin and Sue gave
me a niece and two nephews. Ned and Martha are the
oldest. Little Gilbert was born when Ned was fourteen.

Once, when he was stung on the arm by a wasp, he begged
Sue through his tears to read the Bible to the wasps.

(She moves downstage)

When he was six, he and a little friend gave an animal show
in a tent on the lawn. We asked him what he was going to
do with the pennies they had gathered for admission.

He said, "We're going to give half to the college and half
to the cat!"

When Sue tried to teach him to sing "There's No Place

Like Home," he broke in, "Yes, *there is too!* Over at Aunt Emily's! Over at Aunt Emily's!"

October is a mighty month, for in it, little Gilbert died at eight years. Typhoid.

Not my little Gib!

I see him in the star, and meet his sweet velocity in everything that flies. The little boy we laid away never fluctuates, and his dim society is companion still.

His last cry in delirium was "Open the door, open the door! They're waiting for me!" Quite used to his commandment, his little aunt obeyed.

Who were waiting for him?

All we possess we would give to know. All this and more, though *is* there more, dear friends? More than Love and Death? *Tell me its name!*

> I reason, Earth is short —
> And Anguish — absolute —
> And many hurt,
> But, what of that?
>
> I reason, we could die —
> The best Vitality
> Cannot excel Decay,
> But, what of that?
>
> *(She sits, a robe over her legs)*
>
> I reason, that in Heaven —
> Somehow, it will be even —

Some new Equation, given —
But, what of that?

(She pours tea)

I've had a curious winter, very swift, sometimes sober. I haven't felt well, much — and March amazes me! I didn't think of it, that's all. I hayed a little for the horse two Sundays ago, but it snowed since. Now — the full circle of seasons — spring has come, though delayed. But I would eat evanescence slowly. The lawn is full of south and the odors tangle, and did you hear today for the first the river in the tree? Spring is a happiness so beautiful, so unique, so unexpected, that I don't know what to do with my heart.

(Intimately, to the AUDIENCE*)*

I dare not take it. I dare not leave it. What do you advise?

Eight Saturday noons ago, I was making my black cake with Maggie — dear Maggie — when I saw a great darkness coming, and knew no more until late at night. I woke to find Austin and Vinnie and a strange physician, a Dr. Bigelow, bending over me, and supposed I was dying, or had died, all was so kind and hallowed. I had fainted and lain unconscious for the first time in my life.

(To herself)

What flower did Austin plant on Gilbert's grave? Oh, yes, lilies of the valley. On Father's and Mother's it was — damson-hawthorn. I remember. When it shall come *my* turn, I want a buttercup. Surely the grass will give me *one.* I told Vinnie I want to be carried in a small white coffin

out the back door of Homestead, into the blue, beloved air,
through my garden and Father's barn, and out over the
meadows of Amherst to the burial ground. And for my
requiem —

> That phraseless Melody —
> The Wind does.

Oh, I can hear Vinnie say, "Don't talk like that, Emily."
But *I* say, "Don't be afraid, dear Vinnie, it's only the Fourth
of July."

My earliest friend wrote me the week before he died, "If
I live, I will go to Amherst; if I die, I certainly will."

Ah, democratic Death!

Life is short, isn't it? When *one* is done, I wonder — is
there not another? And then, if God is willing, perhaps
we are neighbors again.

I wonder if I ever dreamed — or if I'm dreaming *now*. I
cannot tell how Eternity seems. It sweeps around me like
a sea. And this world is such a little place, just the red in
the sky, before the sun rises. So let us keep fast hold of
hands, please, that when the birds begin, none of us be
missing!

> The name They dropped upon my face
> With water, in the country church —
> Emily Elizabeth —
> Is finished using, now,
> And They can put it with my Dolls,

My childhood, and the string of spools
I've finished threading.

Because I could not stop for Death —
He kindly stopped for me —
The Carriage held but just Ourselves —
And Immortality.

We slowly drove — He knew no haste
And I had put away
My labor and my leisure too,
For His Civility —

We passed the School, where Children played
Their lessons scarcely done —
We passed the Fields of Gazing Grain —
We passed the Setting Sun —

We paused before a House that seemed
A Swelling of the Ground —
The Roof was scarcely visible —
The Cornice — but a Mound —

Since then — 'tis Centuries — but each
Feels shorter than the Day
I first surmised the Horses' Heads
Were toward Eternity —

(She gets up)

Oh, it's six o'clock! And I promised Vinnie I'd peel the
apples. You know, our visit was easier than I thought it
would be. We very seldom have guests anymore. *Coming,
Vinnie!* But one more thing . . .

(She carries the box of poems downstage center)

This is my letter to the World
That never wrote to Me —
The simple news that Nature told —
With tender Majesty

Her Message is committed
To Hands I cannot see —
For love of Her — Sweet — countrymen —
Judge tenderly — of Me.

Oh, and when you make my cake, please tell me how you like it. And when next we meet — I'll give you my recipe for gingerbread!

(She places the box on the floor)

Gingerbread! Now there's a word to lift your hat to!

Vinnie, I'm here!

*(*EMILY *exits stage left)*